LUDICROUS LIMERICKS

MY BIOGRAPHY - Simon R. Gladdish was born in

Kampala, Uganda in 1957. His family returned to

Britain in 1961, to Reading where he grew up.

Educated at Oxford and Cambridge Universities, he

trained as an English Language Teacher, a

profession which enabled him to work for many

years in Spain, France, Turkey, Tunisia and Kuwait.

Domiciled near Swansea since 1992, he has no

plans to return to the land of his father. In 1999 Poet

Laureate Andrew Motion wrote to him saying, 'I love

the energy of your poems.' Simon strongly believes

that poetry ought to be enjoyable, entertaining and

enlightening. His published books include:-

VICTORIAN VALUES (1995)

BACK TO BASICS (1996)

IMAGES OF ISTANBUL (1997)

SEASONAL AFFECTIVE DISORDER (1997)

ORIGINAL CLICHES (1998)

TORN TICKETS & ROUTINE RETURNS (WITH

RUSTY GLADDISH, 2000)

THE TINY HUNCHBACKED HORSE (WITH VLADIMIR

GROUNINE, 2001)

THE POISONED TUNIC (WITH VLADIMIR

GROUNINE, 2002)

HOMAGE TO EDWARD LEAR (2004)

APHORISMS AFTER OSCAR (2007)

HILLIMERICKS (2008)

TWISTED PROVERBS (2010)

FABLES FROM FONTAINEBLEAU (2013)

THE BOOK OF IRREGULAR SONNETS (2014)

COOKIES OF FORTUNE AND FATE (2015)

CLUMSY CLERIHEWS (2016)

AMAZING ANAGRAMS (2016)

AMERICAN ANAGRAMS (2016)

WILD APHORISMS (2017)

AUSTRALIAN ANAGRAMS (2017)

THE RUBAIYAT OF OMAR KHAYAAM (WITH

ROBERT GRAVES, 2017)

RANDOM THOUGHTS (2018)

SECOND THOUGHTS (2018)

ASSORTED THOUGHTS (2018)

THE RUBAIYAT OF OMAR KHAYYAM (WITH JOHN

HEATH STUBBS, 2019)

VIRTUAL POEMS (2019)

THE LORD'S PRAYER IN 70 LANGUAGES (2019)

THE 10 COMMANDMENTS IN 70 LANGUAGES (2019)

AFTERTHOUGHTS (2020)

LAPTOP POEMS (2020)

LOCKDOWN LAMENTS (2021)

PEPPERMINT AND PINE (2021)

ODE TO A TOAD (2021)

DIGITAL ENCOUNTERS (2021)

FLEETING THOUGHTS (2021)

FRAGMENTED THOUGHTS (2022)

HAPHAZARD THOUGHTS (2022)

THREE GREAT VERSIONS OF THE RUBAIYAT (2022)

LUDICROUS LIMERICKS (2023)

DEDICATION

For my beloved wife Rusty and for both of our extended families.

FOREWORD

According to Wikipedia: 'A limerick is a form of verse, usually humorous and frequently rude, in five-line, predominantly anapestic trimeter with a strict rhyme scheme of AABBA, in which the first, second and fifth line rhyme, while the third and fourth lines are shorter and share a different rhyme. The following is an example:-

The limerick packs laughs anatomical

Into space that is quite economical.

But the good ones I've seen

So seldom are clean

And the clean ones so seldom are comical.'

I was introduced to limericks by my poet father when I was around seven and immediately became hooked. Since then I have read thousands and written over eight hundred original limericks myself. (I don't know of anyone else who has come close to this number.) I like to believe that I have extended the scope of the limerick by adding a few sub-genres. These are Slimericks (Thin Limericks), Climericks (which are a cross between a Clerihew and a Limerick), Quimericks (Erotic Limericks about the fair sex) and Dimericks (Limericks which aren't very good.) All four categories are richly represented here! I hope that you will enjoy reading this book as much as I enjoyed writing it.

(SIMON R. GLADDISH   SWANSEA   SPRING 2023)

'The funniest limericks are obscene.
(There aren't very many that are clean!)
Still, let's not get too quizzical
Or metaphysical -
We don't want to upset the Dean.'

'For her birthday I bought my wife a bottle of Kenzo
But she actually wanted Acqua di Gio;
By the time she was done,
She had called me all the names under the sun -
Sometimes it's best just to go with the flow.'

'Nicola Sturgeon made a mistake;
The Gender Recognition Bill caused her to break.
She was trying to be kind
But I really don't mind -
As a unionist, it's a victory I'll take.'

'Nicola Sturgeon
Needed a surgeon
To remove her fists
From the Scottish Nationalists
But now a sort of human being is emergin'.

'Raquel Welch's
Ancestry was Welsh.
Or if it wasn't, it should have been;
She's the best-looking woman I've ever seen
Apart from the starlet Arabella Squelch.'

'Mr McCartney is very rich.
He started out without a stitch
But now he is a billionaire;
It's just so unfair
That others must sleep in a ditch.'

'It costs around 50p
To press a CD;
So why is Taylor Swift still
Demanding thirteen quid
For her Midnights LP?'

'I was dead beat,
Out on my feet;
I felt tired
And uninspired
So I crawled beneath the cotton sheet.'

'There are crystals in the sky
 Or is it something in my eye?
 There are milky bars
 And things called stars
 But we never know the reason why.'

'She was a typist
 Who forgave her rapist;
 Everyone thought she was mad
 Because the man was very bad,
 Claiming he had urges that he could not resist.'

'I heard nothing
 But my wife heard her phone ping;
 It was her daughter
 Saying she ought to
 Give her a ring.'

'Life isn't neat
 And history doesn't repeat
 Though I suppose
 That in a way it does
 With different metric feet.'

'There was a young girl named Brianna
Who was beaten to death with a spanner.
The day that she died
We just stood there and cried
And wished we could move to Montana.'

Toxic masculinity
Has a certain currency;
I've known some serious bastards in my time
But no longer traffic with subhuman slime
And concentrate on those touched by divinity.'

'I view the world like an American evangelist
Or more precisely through the eyes of Jesus Christ.
Everybody takes the piss
But what they're missing is this:
One day we'll be in Heaven when they are dust and ice.'

'I met Margaret Thatcher once;
She was about five feet from her toes to her bonce
But when she grabbed her handbag,
Grown men's hearts began to sag.
I said Hello and sat politely on the fence.'

'I used to be a royalist but I'm not any more.
I now find The Palace a bit of a bore.
They're as rich as Queen Bess
And they couldn't care less
About people like us or the widow next door.'

'Gherkins are not to everyone's taste
But they are to mine. I think it's a waste
If you pick them out of your salad
And moan that you'd rather have mallard
Or something common like salmon paste.'

'Joe Biden
Appears to be hidin'
Somethin'. I think it's his brain
But then again
My own is slidin'.

'She was shocked at the amount
Fraudsters had removed from her account
So she phoned the Halifax
Who admitted they'd been lax
And eventually refunded every pound.'

'I am the man who's dressed in black;
 I wear a black shirt on my back;
 I wear black clothes
 From my nose to my toes
 Plus an extremely dark and dirty mac.'

'What can I say?
 I don't have five a day;
 I like parsnips and potatoes,
 Turnips and tomatoes
 But the T-bone steaks keep getting in the way!'

'My wife and I worked in Istanbul for a year
 So when the earthquake struck, we felt the fear;
 We made a contribution
 To an international solution
 And also blinked back many a bitter tear.'

'It seems the earth,
 Soon after birth
 (For our original sin)
 Can swallow us like aspirin -
 Our lives are roughly what the rats' are worth.'

'It's so unwise
 To recycle lies;
 Just tell the truth
 To Tom and Ruth
 And claim the cosmic prize.'

'One plus six is seven
 And two plus nine's eleven;
 If you don't change your behaviour
 And accept Jesus as your saviour,
 It's unlikely you will ever enter Heaven.'

'Charles the First
 Felt a raging thirst
 But when he rose from his bed
 Lost his royal head;
 I suppose the poor fellow was cursed.'

'Doctor Foster
 Was a total impostor;
 He did complex operations
 On his patients and relations
 And performed pretty well on his roster.'

'Isn't it funny
How God still needs money.
The Vatican and evangelists
Are rattling their cans for the Eucharist.
(Forget the land flowing with milk and honey.)

'An earthquake
Makes the ground shake;
It's terrible
And horrible
And makes everything break.'

'On Twitter I have troughs and spikes,
I get a lot of looks but not too many likes;
I'm an occasional drinker
And an independent thinker
So if you don't appreciate my stuff, get on your bikes!'

'Lady Godiva
Lost a fresh fiver;
Her skin was entirely bare,
She couldn't find it anywhere
And may have to employ a muff diver.'

'I can't help feeling you've got some issues
With your crocodile tears and Kleenex tissues;
I never meant to hurt you,
Much less to desert you -
If only donkeys were horses and good intentions were wishes.'

'Elvis Costello
Knows how to bellow;
In car, train or bar
He plays his guitar
But never quite mastered the cello.'

'Johnny Cash
Had a massive smash
In 1969
With 'I Walk The Line'
(He was cool without being overly brash.)

'Sometimes in life we feel we cannot win;
We have insufficient money coming in.
When you've nothing in your cup
And your debts are piling up,
The best thing is to bear it with a grin.'

'We have a small kitten called Minky
Who's incredibly smart, cute and dinky;
He's extremely affectionate
And thinks being stroked is great
But when he gets in his tray, he's quite stinky!'

'There's a lot to be said
For being in bed;
Deliberately choosing
Relaxing and snoozing
And dreaming and snoring - said Fred.'

'I read the Runes
(The Looney Tunes.)
They said I'd be comfortable but never rich
(Death's not much fun and life's a bitch!)
And to expect improvements around June.'

'I read the Tarot cards
(The whole nine yards!)
They said that I would die one day
(I guess I knew that anyway)
And, late in life, would be a famous bard.'

'I have to be blunt
About Russia's wee runt;
Putin's invaded Ukraine
Causing terror and pain -
He's a monumental and massive affront!'

'Why is word
Only one letter away from world and sword?
I can confidently swear
There's a connection there -
All three words are connected by a silver cord.'

'I was shocked to see my soul
Disappear down a black hole.
Everything turned black;
I have got to get it back
And from now on, that's my goal.'

'If you complain
You will remain
Exactly where you are -
Within this seedy bar
(Without enough to buy a jar)
Amid a world of pain.'

'Tomorrow begins today.
 Good things come my way.
 Feel the fear and do it anyway.
 Fill your life with colour, not with grey.
 If all else fails, get on your bended knees and pray.'

'There is an evangelist called Julie Green
 Who's the craziest chick you've ever seen;
 She claims the real Joe Biden's dead
 And his replacement's being led
 By Barack Obama, as he had always been.'

'In Britain we favour the plucky underdog,
 The socially-disadvantaged frog;
 We shout our encouragement
 As they crawl along the tunnel of advancement
 Then stamp on them
 As they struggle to emerge from the bog.'

'David Icke
 Is somebody I rather like;
 It is hard to resist
 Such a charming conspiracy theorist,
 (He is lucky he wasn't called Mike.)'

'Our Poet Laureate Arnie
Resembles Paul McCartney;
A people-pleasing,
Language-teasing
Heir to Hughes and Heaney.'

'Don Paterson
Resembles John Lennon;
A tortured genius
(Obsessed with his penius)
He really divides poetic opinion.'

'Today the buildings went jerky
When there was a terrible earthquake in Turkey;
I have read
There's over three thousand dead
Although other details are murky.'

'I lost another tooth today;
That makes around a dozen lost to decay.
I'm not completely bereft,
I've still got a handful left
And just pray that the remaining ones will stay.'

'The school was secretly thrilled
 When the headmistress was killed;
 The husband was guilty,
 The crime scene was filthy
 And all the front pages were filled.'

'I spent this afternoon playing Wet Wet Wet
 Who are as good as a band can get;
 I Love Is All Around me
 And Sweet Little Mystery
 And Wishing I Was Lucky is the best one yet.'

'I used to live on the seventh floor
 But I don't any more.
 It was a bitter blow
 When I fell out of the open window
 (I'm writing this from Heaven and I still feel slightly sore.)'

'You line them all up in a row
 And then you flick the first domino;
 Within a sec-
 ond they have hit the deck
 Because they've nowhere else to go.'

'If you own some property,
 You avoid the sting of poverty;
 If you're wealthy,
 Healthy, stealthy,
 You know how to do things properly.'

'Caroline Cory
 Is not a Tory;
 She's a beautiful soul
 Who tells us the whole
 History of our human story.'

'Jackie Kay
 Is very gay;
 She dislikes sex with men
 But then again,
 Her son was born this way.'

'Dan Biggar
 Is a better kicker
 Than Owen Farrell
 Who's a barrel
 Of laughs but a goal-misser.'

'I wanted Wales to win but they lost.
I wanted England to win but they tossed
Away an easy victory against the Jocks;
The game was one of knocks and shocks
Leaving their dispirited supporters to count the cost.'

'When Ireland play rugby against Wales,
They always choose their toughest males;
I will wear a massive grin
If Wales manages to win
So let us pray they won't get crushed like snails.'

'I used to know a lake
That was stuffed with hake;
On the other hand I oughter
Point out that hake prefer salt water
So I may have made a mistake.'

'I washed up in a sink
Which I think was made of zinc;
It had a shiny tap
That opened with a snap
But the water was unfit to drink.'

'Grip the earth with your toes.
 Breathe in through your nose.
 Exhale through your mouth.
 Look North and then South.
 Smell the coffee and the rose.'

'Of all the colours I've seen,
 My favourite colour is green;
 I also love blue
 And vermilion too
 But I've liked green since I was a teen.'

'My younger brother
 Has recently become a mother;
 I didn't know a thing
 About his transitioning
 But I wish him all the best as 'Cat Carruthers.'

'We have to support Ukraine
 Again and again and again;
 If Russia wins
 Then for our sins
 We'll lose our skins
 So we have to support Ukraine!'

'If you suffer from addiction,
 You will probably face eviction;
 You'll be out on the street
 With a dog at your feet
 Plus a police conviction.'

'The internet was supposed to set us free
 But now we live in an attention economy;
 If you produce your boobs
 On Tik Tok or You Tube,
 You will be famous for a minute or three.'

'Our neighbour wrecked our roof
 But we don't have too much proof.
 It cost a grand to fix;
 I wish that I could nix
 The swine and that's the truth.'

'Today the teachers went on strike.
 Is it their pupils they don't like?
 Anyway, they used their holiday
 To demand far more pay
 And strenuously deny they were taking the Mike.'

'Today the nurses went on strike.
Is it their patients they dislike?
Anyway, they used their holiday
To demand far more pay
And strenuously deny they were taking the Mike.'

'Medicine was made easier by Obama
But madness means money for Big Pharma;
When you fall quite ill
They've always got the right pill
And seem never to question their karma.'

'I noticed that she
Had got stuck in a tree;
Though I could barely see her
I did my best to free her
Then rewarded us both with a nice cup of tea.'

'All over this planet
Are people called Janet
And Jason and Jane
And Wanda and Wayne
(The last needs a campaign to ban it!)'

'Tomorrow and today
Everyone's on strike for better pay
But if Rishi doesn't get a grip,
Then inflation's going to rip
And we'll all be far worse off in every way.'

'When we had our daughter
We decided on 'Elektra';
To our eternal shame
She didn't like her name
And now insists on being called 'Alexa'.

'It's not hard to detect
Mental patients suffering neglect;
It takes real guts
To admit you're nuts
So please show them some respect.'

'Every year we have a proper Christmas tree
With pine-green needles fresh as they can be;
After a month or so
I toss it through the window
Which is rather sad, we all agree.'

'Horatio isn't bad
Although he did go slightly mad;
After smoking too much dope
He believed he was the Pope
But he's still a lovely lad.'

'Is that the money, honey?
No, darling, it's the honey money.
What's the difference?
Honey has a sweeter scent.
Will you please cease trying to be funny, honey!

'I tried playing snooker but I didn't have a clue
And, more to the point, I didn't have a cue;
It's hard to hit those balls
When you're wearing just your smalls
And you're colour-blind and can't make out the blue.'

'The audience squeals.
The little short-arse in the high-heels
Pounds the piano until it groans;
The audience moans.
The little short-arse signs another deal.'

'I am growing older
With a boulder on my shoulder
Which is almost as good as a pip
And much better than a chip;
I rip the last page from my folder.'

'Boy, you ain't got a lick o' sense!
As I get older I prize competence;
The ability to lay bricks
Or simply to fix
A shattered item or a broken fence.'

'Outside it's sleeting.
Fame is fleeting.
Fortune's returning.
My hands are burning.
I turn down the heating.'

'Jacob Rees-Mogg, the notorious sleeper,
Said Brexit would make everything cheaper;
The truth is, of course,
Things have gotten much worse
And Rees-Mogg has become the grim reaper.'

'A vast number of commentators carp
About BBC boss Richard Sharp;
It is not a deal-breaker
(He's much better than Dacre!)
So come on guys, please cut all the crap.'

'Our neighbour broke our roof
But we didn't have much proof
So in order to keep the peace
We didn't call the police
To report his cloven hoof.'

'At college I had a damn good education;
I've also been blessed with an imagination.
I've written forty books -
Come on and take a look!
And could you lend me a few bob for recreation?'

'When I was at college I stole traffic cones
And also decided to join 'Skull & Bones';
It was foolish and rash
As they took all my cash
And when I woke up, felt depressed and alone.'

'Around our former garden, at the edge
Stood an impressive and imposing high beech hedge;
It was difficult to police,
The dog shat underneath
And the greenfly named the leaves their favourite veg.'

'Donald Trump
Is a grump,
Trying to control the southern border
With his Narcissistic Personality Disorder -
What a chump!'

'We can choose to be good or bad.
We can choose to be happy or sad.
We can choose to be pleasant and witty
Or otherwise nothing but shitty;
We can choose to be moderate or mad.'

'He was as mad as a bag of frogs
But continued to keep careful logs;
He was a resourceful fella
Who later wrote a bestseller
Which was better than Jacob Rees-Mogg's.'

'There was a young fellow called Horace
Who altered his first name to Boris
But after thinking a bit,
He thought Boris was shit
So he decided to call himself Maurice.'

'We can choose to be good or evil.
We can choose to be crooked or level.
God gave us free will
And we should have it still -
We can either serve God or the devil.'

'When you walk past our house there's a smell
Given off by our neighbour from hell;
He has damaged our roof
But there isn't much proof
So we continue as though all is well.'

'When I tried to buy a toy
I was asked - Are you a local boy?
This was a question I'd been dreading
As I'd basically been brought up in Reading.
Of course, I answered, My surname's Jenkins
And my first name's Roy.'

'I'm starting to think my girlfriend is a spy;
She speaks the Russian language better than I.
She knows German, Spanish, Greek
And tends to vanish every week
And I met her whilst at Cambridge. I won't lie.'

'I'm anxious to hear
What will happen this year:
Wars and rumours of wars,
Sores and tumours and scores
Of rational reasons to ratchet up our fear.'

'Today the scaffolders arrived;
They were wiry, tough and alive.
It took them over an hour
To build their tower
Before they left with a high-five.'

'Virgos are a pedantic lot
Who question every tittle and jot;
They love nit-picking and hair-splitting,
Pointless distinctions and bullshitting
And often talk complete and utter rot.'

'There was an old fellow named Don
 Who tended to drone on and on;
 Even when he was point-scoring,
 He was still pretty boring
 Although not quite as boring as Ron.'

'Last night I dreamt that I was given two
 Wristwatches which were turquoise blue;
 I wore them on my wrist
 And then got soundly pissed
 And lost them between the circus and the zoo.'

'Maybe it's worthy of mention,
 I spent today listening to Fairport Convention;
 It has to be said
 That they're still pretty good
 Although why is beyond comprehension.'

'As a child I did origami,
 Only breaking off for a slice of salami;
 I made monkeys and men,
 Peacocks and hens
 And my parents both thought I was barmy.'

'By hook or by crook,
 Take a leaf from my book;
 You will dine like a prince
 (On potatoes and mince!)
 If you marry a cook.'

'There was a young thing called Diane
 Who could probably attract any man;
 Her eyes were bright blue
 In a luminous hue
 And her skin wore a light golden tan.'

'Poets are tight.
 Poets think they're right.
 Poets are dumb.
 Poets are scum
 And their poetry is shite!'

'There is a comedienne called Shappi
 Whose jokes are both witty and snappy;
 She fled from Iran
 With a credible plan
 To grow up successful and happy.'

'Poets have bored me.
Poets have ignored me.
Poets have impressed me.
Poets have distressed me
But poets have rarely, if ever, restored me.'

'I spent three months on an isle;
I did it to hone my style
But what I achieved
Was not well-received
And thrown in the remainder pile.'

'There was a young fellow named Tate
Who made a good living from hate
Till the Romanian police
Made his activities cease
Though some said it had happened too late.'

'Some things are completely absurd,
Like the day that I stepped in a turd;
The smell it was - phew, man! -
I thought it looked human
Till a dog's merry laughter I heard.'

'If there's one thing we really don't like,
It's when unions go out on strike;
You can't catch a train,
A bus or a plane -
No wonder it gives us the spike!'

'The advantages of civilisation
Are intelligent conversation
And Chinese food
And burnished wood
And birthday celebrations.'

'For most of his life he was straight
But then turned queer at eighty-eight;
When asked to explain,
He said - I fancied a change
Before it was far too late!'

'She spent three months on Bleaker
Where she felt her self-worth growing weaker;
She was alone,
As alone as a stone
Without either cell phone or speaker.'

'With a forced grin
 I did the bins;
 There was a ton
 Of post-Christmas shite
 To throw out
 For my sins.'

'He couldn't read or write
 But he could fight;
 He was a dangerous man
 With many notches on his gun -
 In short, he was a complete and utter shite!'

'I was a tailor
 And then a sailor;
 I went to sea
 Aged forty-three
 As my life was a total failure.'

'On Christmas Eve
 I believe
 We opened our present
 (Which was very pleasant!)
 I got a sieve.'

'In Afghanistan
 The Taliban
 Have prevented women
 From being a citizen
 Like a man.'

'Yesterday I got dead drunk,
 As drunk as an elephant's trunk;
 I was drinking quite quick
 Till I felt pretty sick
 And fell head-first right into my bunk.'

'There was a young rocker named Springsteen
 (Not as good as Roy Orbison but could still scream!)
 This long afternoon
 I've played him again
 And realised his songs are still evergreen.'

I've known some lonesome days
 (Without your loving gaze)
 But since you've been home again
 You've anaesthetised my pain
 And shown me a way out of the maze.' (For Rusty)

'For three years he wanted to commit suicide
 Though he thought he could be a writer if he tried;
 His first book was a smash
 Which brought him loads of cash -
 Now he's grateful and relieved he hasn't died.'

'Have no fear,
 Keir is here!
 Your friendly neighbour,
 The leader of Labour
 Will be in power next year.'

'Whatever we eat
 We later excrete;
 There's no question
 That our digestion
 Is pretty neat.'

'If you're thinking of taking a train,
 Then you're going to suffer the strain;
 It is almost unbelievable
 That the trains are less reliable
 Here than they are in Ukraine.'

'Every different tribe
Has its own distinctive vibe.
That's what they say
But who are 'they'?
(This is not a diatribe.)

'You've survived everything you've been through
And you will survive this too.
Don't call me that
(You stupid twat!)
I'm only trying to encourage you.'

'First of all I needed a pee
And then I accidentally peed on my knee;
I felt quite sad
But it didn't smell too bad -
I realised there are far worse things than wee.'

'These times are disjointed
So we're often disappointed
But it doesn't have to be like this;
We can still achieve a state of bliss
And feel a bit anointed.'

'I think I need a nap.
My mental health is crap.
I've got a million things to do;
I cannot find my other shoe
And feel as though I'm in a trap.'

'We will hold his feet to the fire!
We will take him right up to the wire!
But how can Mark Rowley
(Especially solely)
Make sure the Met's standards are higher?

'There's a bit of a mess at the Met
With some coppers as bent as they get;
I don't envy their Chief
Who has nothing but grief
And a number of rapists to net.'

'My wife came up quite late
Which meant I had to wait
For the pleasance
Of her presence
In the water bed where we luxuriate.'

'I'm a head-in-sand person;
 I'm a head-in-hands person.
 Very few can faster
 Imagine a disaster -
 I'm a someone no-one-understands person.'

'Hanif fell and found his head
 Wedged between the wall and the bed;
 He couldn't move and was forced to wait
 Until a nurse came. Though he could dictate
 And thankfully is still widely read.'

'After a bit of a think,
 Elon Musk sent Ukraine his Starlink;
 An unusual sell
 But it's working so well
 That the Russians are now on the brink.'

'I got in a muddle
 And needed a cuddle;
 My wife said - Go away!
 So I started to pray
 And then went and lay in a puddle.'

'There was a young lady named Laura
Who had a kid sister called Flora;
Flora was pretty
But Laura was gritty
And refused to obey others' orders.'

'I enter the lounge with a sinking heart;
The kittens are tearing the place apart.
Their mum (asleep on a chair!)
Clearly couldn't care
As she alternates purrs, snores and farts.'

'I played the National Lottery
Together with my coterie;
We'd had some fun
But hadn't won
So why did I feel so grottery?'

'My favourite substance is honey
And my seventh favourite is money;
That's probably why
I'm as poor as a fly
And my garret is not very sunny.'

'There was an old fellow called Roger
Who spent fifty years as a lodger
And his landlady's brood
(Some bad and some good)
Were all the result of his todger.'

'There was a young fellow named Bjorn
Who had an addiction to porn;
Eyes fixed on a screen,
He would watch things obscene
Whilst subduing his priapic horn.'

'There's a lot of disorder
Down at the border
With barely surviving
Migrants arriving
And the Tories all crying blue murder!'

'There was a young princeling named Harry
Who one day decided to marry
An American actress
Who made him feel less helpless
By ordering him not to worry.'

'A Managing Director named Elon
Has allegedly lost 165 billion;
After hearing this story,
One can't help but feel sorry
But I bet he's still got a few million.'

'If I stay as still as can be,
The kitten will sit on my knee
But when I move
Or try to improve
My position, he jumps off the settee.'

'I hear the pages turning
And wonder what it is you're learning;
I use my hooks
To grab your books
And pile them up for burning.'

'I tolerate the taste
Of ancient salmon-paste;
When my wife asks why,
I soon reply -
It saves a lot of waste.'

'There was a young fellow named Jonah
Who married a woman called Mona;
On their wedding night
He gave her a fright
When he showed her the size of his boner.'

'You said that my conclusion
Was probably an illusion;
I took another look
At my scientific book
And realised life is nothing but confusion.'

'He made the decision
To medically transition;
His carrot was cut
Along with his nuts
But now he regrets his revision.'

'Is the earth ethereal
Or is it just material?
Maybe it's both -
By the way, why are you so loath
To share your mint imperials?'

'Nikola Tesla had his passions
And, sadly, also his obsessions;
His idea of religion
Was communing with pigeons
Who helped him create his inventions.'

'My brother is a pessimist
But I was born an optimist;
My glass is half-full,
And the economy's bull
Which is why I became an artiste.'

'Does the 'deep state' exist?
Are we called to resist?
I'll have to have a think,
Pour myself another drink
And probably get pissed!'

'If you make money for the company,
You're contributing to the economy
Though I'd rather live in a cave
Than be a wage-slave
For what's a life worth without liberty?'

'If we ever become too smart
The Powers that Be will start
To control and confuse us,
Mislead and abuse us,
Divide us and keep us apart.'

'Sending money out I made a mess
Of the destination address;
It never arrived -
I would not have survived
Without my wife's tender caress.'

'Sending money out I made a mess
Of the destination address;
It never arrived,
I barely survived
And now envy the beast at Loch Ness.'

'She has a healthy appetite,
In fact, she eats both day and night;
As for putting on weight,
Please don't mention it, mate,
But her pants are becoming quite tight.'

'A Union leader named Lynch
 Thought winning his strike was a cinch;
 His features were saturnine
 As he gurned on the picket line -
 Now everyone calls him 'The Grinch.'

'As I approach seventy
 I'm becoming more sedentary;
 I don't look too great -
 I've put on some weight
 And my missus has sent me to Coventry.'

'Is he gay?
 It's hard to say;
 He's certainly handsome
 And earns a king's ransom -
 So I suppose it doesn't matter, either way.'

'How frightened must you be
 To grab your kids and flee?
 The Russian bombs are falling
 And the carnage is appalling -
 It's the price Ukraine is paying for Europe to be free.'

'I remember when Germaine Greer said
That 'Me Too' had come to a head;
I thought she was wrong
But it wasn't too long
Before it was dying or dead.'

'I was starting to experience the tension
Of waiting for years for my pension;
It's now on the way
But suffice it to say
That money's still too tight to mention.'

'There was a young artist named Gill
Who lived for a sexual thrill;
He shagged his sisters, his daughters,
His dog and the porters -
Indeed, anything with an opening to fill.'

'There is a young fellow named Charles
Who owns an Alsatian that snarls;
He threw it a stick,
Then gave it a kick
And is now hiding somewhere in Wales.'

'There was a young fellow called Sean
 Who was wondering why he'd been born;
 He thought it so odd
 That he tried asking God
 Who responded with withering scorn.'

'Adam was alone in the Garden
 And soon felt his genitals harden;
 He turned on his side,
 Some firm pressure applied,
 And then begged the Almighty for pardon.'

'Anacondas are now all the rage
 But I've had to put mine in a cage;
 He sank his fangs in my wife
 And ended her life
 Which has somewhat soured my old age.'

'My girlfriend declared the other day
 That she had decided to go gay;
 She took all my things,
 My records and rings,
 And left me with huge bills to pay.'

'In America, thanks to the 2nd Amendment,
Guns are easier to buy than cement;
You can then visit a store
And try to shoot more
Than the last nutter whose ammo was spent.'

'The devil has ceased to be myth
And has taken the name of Mark Smith;
An innocent name
But a dangerous game -
I think that he'th taking the pith.'

'There was a young goalie named Hope
Who posed in the nude with a rope
But in less than a week
The photos were leaked
And now they're as common as soap.'

'There was a film mogul called Harvey
Who, to put it politely, was pervy;
His principal fault
Was sexual assault
Made worse by the fact he had scurvy.'

'There was a footballer called Wayne
Who was starting to suffer the strain
Of getting down on all fours
To service old whores
Again and again and again.'

'I don't want you thinking I'm Wayne;
My name's Simon. I hope that that's plain.
He's rich and I'm poor,
He's fit and I'm sure
My old knees couldn't cope with the pain.'

'There once was an elderly whore
Who enjoyed making love on the floor
Though her unbridled passion
To go doggie-fashion
Is becoming a bit of a bore!'

'I suppose that I must have enjoyed
Reading the works of Sig Freud;
They lifted the lid
On my ego and id -
My wife thinks I'm under-employed.'

'A young mathematician named Tim
Sometimes went out on a limb;
He said - Darling Tess,
Would you please undress?
Today I'm counting the hairs on your quim.'

'A woman from Bexhill-on-Sea
Was itching, one day, for a pee.
To a chorus of chants
She lowered her pants
And started to piss copiously.'

There was a young lady of Perth
Prone to low self-esteem and self worth.
She said to her shrink,
'I'm fat, ugly and stink,'
Whilst her mother exploded with mirth.

'I think that I've finished my book;
I hope that you're taking a look.
It's okay to laugh
In your bed or the bath -
You'd be amazed at the effort it took!'

(COPYRIGHT   SIMON R GLADDISH   2023)

Printed in Great Britain
by Amazon